Change careers
successfully

Change careers successfully

How to make a job switch work for you

A & C Black • London

First published in 2008 by
A & C Black Publishers Ltd
38 Soho Square
London W1D 3HB
www.acblack.com

Text copyright © A & C Black Publishers Ltd 2008

Cover image © Martin Shovel
www.creativityworks.net

A CIP record for this book is available from the British Library.

ISBN 978-0-7136-8844-3

Design by Fiona Pike, Pike Design, Winchester
Typeset by RefineCatch Limited, Bungay, Suffolk
Printed in Spain by Graphycems

This book is produced using paper that is made from wood grown in
managed, sustainable forests. It is natural, renewable and recyclable.
The logging and manufacturing processes conform to the environmental
regulations of the country of origin.

Contents

Are you ready to switch careers?

Answer these questions and work out your score, then read the guidance points overleaf for advice on how take a change of direction at work.

Are you clear about your personal strengths and weaknesses?
a) I'm not really sure… If I'm bad at something I don't usually identify it as a weakness until someone tells me.
b) Sort of. I haven't sat down and identified them all, but am fairly clear on what they are.
c) Yes, I know exactly what I'm good at and what I can't do.

For you, the most important aspect of work is…?
a) The money. As long as it pays the bills I'm not bothered what I do.
b) Being able to do it. As long as I am paid enough and get the occasional sense of satisfaction I'm content.
c) Satisfaction. I need to be completely happy with my job and what it consists of, this has a huge impact on my work ethic.

How high is your tolerance for uncertainty and insecurity?

a) Pretty low! I get scared by the idea of not having a solid income!
b) Ok. I wouldn't immediately freak out, but I couldn't stand it in the long term.
c) Good. I always look on the positive side and enjoy taking calculated risks.

When confronted with a challenge you...

a) Try and avoid it as much as possible.
b) Try to pass it off onto someone else but still make a small contribution.
c) Rise to it! I love challenges and as long as I'm motivated nothing is too much trouble!

How would you feel about making a lateral move within your present company, rather than moving to a new one?

a) Unexcited. What good would it do?
b) I worry about any related office politics.
c) Quite positive! I may learn a lot without the upheaval of trying out a new employer.

Can you see the benefits of a portfolio career?

a) Not really. Wouldn't it just look like I can't stick at any-thing?
b) Yes, but I feel a bit nervous about it.
c) I think it suits today's working patterns, so yes!

Do you keep up to speed with changes in your chosen industry?

a) Who has time for that?

b) I try to, but I'm only really aware of how they related to the company I work for.

c) Absolutely: the Internet is a boon for that.

When you start a new job, how do you build new relationships with others?

a) I like to show them who's boss. I'm a big fan of the 'new broom' approach!

b) I find it helps to explain what I did in my previous job.

c) For the first week or so, I tend to listen to my new colleagues to find out as much as I can about the new company's culture and approach, so that I know how to start filtering my changes through.

a = 1, b = 2, c = 3 Now add up your scores!

■ **8–14:** Taking the time to think carefully about what you want from your career can reap many rewards. You seem a little confused at the moment, but chapter 1 will help you work out how you feel about your current job and whether you're going through a short-term blip or ready to make a bigger change.

■ **15–19:** You are already on the right lines, but need to concentrate your efforts a bit more to get the results you're after. If you know you're ready to change careers, spend as much time as you can researching the opportunities out there for you and your skills:

chapters 2 and 5 will be very helpful here. The portfolio career isn't something to be sniffed at if you want to pursue several avenues: turn to chapter 7.

■ **20–24:** Your preparation work will have meant that you now have a clear idea of what you're aiming at. To learn from colleagues in other departments if you're not yet ready to leave your existing employer, a lateral move may work for you — see chapter 8. Once you've got the job of your dreams in an exciting new industry, however, turn to chapter 9 for advice on how to make the right sort of impact in your first week. Good luck!

1
Making sure you're in the right job

The last time many of us thought seriously about our careers was at school or university. We set out on our career paths with a clear starting point and some idea of what we might move on to, but had a complete blank about what might come after. If you find yourself at a career crossroads, it's time to take action and to manage your career actively—to make sure you're getting the most from it, both financially and in terms of your personal development.

It's rare these days for employers to provide anyone with career-long job security, so it's up to you to craft your own career strategies, and manage them carefully. The alternative? Ending up on the sidelines while opportunities pass you by. This book will help you avoid languishing in the career doldrums and this chapter offers help in deciding whether a career change is for you: you need to assess your present situation, and decide whether you're really heading for where you want to be.

Step one: Stop and think

It's human nature to wonder, regardless of what we happen to be doing, whether we ought in fact to be doing something else. This is particularly the case with jobs; most people spend at least some of their working life questioning themselves and their careers, and speculating about whether there are other occupations 'out there' which might make better use of their time and efforts.

If you feel you've reached an impasse, perhaps because outside factors have forced you to stop and think, it is important to ask yourself:

- Would I be happy to continue what I'm doing for the rest of my working life?
- What do I really want to do?
- How will I make the transition?

As with most things, it helps to analyse the situation objectively. A job is made up of many elements—it's not just the actual day-to-day work—and it's the combination of these elements that makes it what you want to do, or otherwise. Your *skills*, of course, are fundamental to what you do, but are these the same as your *strengths*? And what about your values? Then there's the company you work for. . . is it the right size, in the right industry sector, with the right culture? Finally, there are the questions about who you work with, what your boss is like, whether you have acceptable levels of responsibility, what kind of pay and benefits you receive, and so on and so forth.

By looking at all these factors, you can work out whether your job is suitable for you, and if not, start thinking about what needs to be put right.

Step two: Identify your areas of interest

First and foremost, if you're not interested in what you're doing, you're never going to be able to put your heart into your work. So if your company, industry, subject, or sector doesn't engage you, think about going back to basics and identify what does.

Is there a **topic, issue, or activity** that you've enjoyed or had in your mind for a long time—art, maths, helping others, science, construction or the environment, for example?

Or does a **specific job** attract you—possibly something that you've dismissed in the past for some reason, or one based on something that you do as a hobby? Maybe you'd like to be a website designer, financial adviser, music teacher, painter/decorator, or landscape gardener, for instance?

Or perhaps there's a **specific industry** that fascinates you—advertising, manufacturing, health care, electronics, entertainment, whatever—that you could explore further. Any area that excites your curiosity or makes you want to know more is a good place to start!

Step three: Pinpoint your strengths

Once you've settled on an area of interest, the most important aspect of any job is whether it makes the best use of your individual strengths. If it does, many of the other elements of satisfactory employment— self-fulfilment, motivation, a sense of achievement, and so on—fall naturally into place. So the first thing to do is to assess your strengths, and seriously consider whether or not you're using these in your current position.

Your strengths can be defined as the areas where your interests and your abilities overlap; in other words, the business activities that you both like *and* are good at. The two aren't necessarily the same!

Take a look at the table below and, being as honest as you can, put ticks against the activities you are interested in, and then against the ones you're good at. The rows where you get ticks in both 'Interest' and 'Ability' are your main strengths. You may find there are some surprises in your results. The list of activities is by no means exhaustive, so add in any others that apply particularly to you.

Interest	Activities	Ability
	Research	
	Analysis	
	Interpretation	
	Problem-solving	
	Budgeting	
	Planning	
	Process management	
	Leadership	
	Decision-making	
	Follow through	
	Administration	
	Mentoring	
	Innovation	
	Imagination	
	Vision	
	Project management	
	Empathy	
	Listening	
	Written presentation	
	Verbal presentation	

Interest	Activities	Ability
	Negotiation	
	Initiative	
	Flexibility	
	Team working	
	Facilitating	
	Installing	
	Operating	

Once you've identified your strengths, consider whether and how you're using them in your job:

- Could you be doing more with them?
- Are there other areas of the organisation which might benefit from them?
- Could you take on different responsibilities, or would a shift in the focus of your job suit you better?

If you feel that you've more to offer, try talking to your boss—any sensible employer will understand the benefits of making the most of their employees' strengths, and will value people who are proactive in the way they approach their work.

TOP TIP
Unless you know deep-down that you're going to move on, make sure you use positive language when you broach this issue with your boss, and be as upbeat as you can so that you don't panic him or her into thinking that you're going to leave immediately.

Being good at what you do doesn't necessarily mean that you're in the right job. There's more to doing a job than simply being able to fulfil the requirements. You could be a very good builder because you're physically strong and fit, but you may have the soul of a philosopher, or a secret yearning to be a garden designer. It's when your interests and abilities coincide that you find yourself in the ideal job. That said, however, if you're happy in your work and don't feel the need to stretch yourself in other directions, you probably *are* in the right job—at least for the time being.

As every person has many facets to his or her personality, most people could do any of a number of different jobs and be equally happy and satisfied. Broadly speaking, however, there are four main areas of personality which need to be fulfilled within a work context for people to be content with their job. These are:

■ areas of interest
■ job strengths

- behaviour under normal and stress conditions
- social perceptions and compatibility with others

If you find that you've got a mismatch between any of these four and the job you are doing, it's unlikely that you'll be comfortable in that job.

Step four: Consider the organisation you work for

A good match between your strengths and the work you are doing proves that you are in the right *type* of job. But is it in the right place? For example, you could be an accountant in a big blue-chip corporation, when really you'd be happiest running the finances for a small family-run firm.

Think about the organisation you work for. How big is it? Would you prefer to work with more or fewer people? Apart from size, here's a list of other factors you might consider:

- public/private sector
- profit/non-profit
- national/multinational
- academic
- product/service
- central/decentralised
- financial condition

- political climate
- company growth (current and future)
- stability
- reputation
- market dependency
- profitability
- vulnerability to takeover

Step five: Think about your rewards

Now assess the rewards you receive for the work you do. While these shouldn't necessarily be the most important aspect of your job, obviously you need to have a reasonable income, benefits, and so on. This is even more the case if your circumstances mean that you require a certain level of income or security—if you have children, for example, or a mortgage.

Remember that it's not just salary that should be considered—other benefits are equally as important. A pension, life and disability insurance, health benefits, or a severance package could be vital if you have a family; a bonus scheme or other performance incentive might be a prime motivator if you're the kind of person who likes to have targets. If you're expected to travel or relocate, what provision is made for moving expenses, temporary living costs, or housing subsidy? Does the holiday entitlement give you enough time with your children? What about flexible working, or study leave?

Step six: Evaluate yourself

Then there's your own personality to consider. It's
extremely stressful to have to try to fill a role that
simply isn't 'you'. Much of this comes down to your
own personal values, but useful areas to examine are as
follows:

■ **interpersonal.** Do you like working with other
people? Is it essential to you that colleagues are also
friends?

■ **responsibility.** How much do you like? Do you prefer
to manage, or would you rather be managed?

■ **pressure.** A high-stress hospital ward or newspaper or
magazine office wouldn't suit someone who likes quiet
routine work. How much pressure can you cope with?
Are you good with deadlines?

■ **potential.** Are you a high-flier with ambitions for regular
promotion, or do you want a steady job that pays just
enough to support your family?

■ **compatibility with lifestyle.** Do you have hobbies
or non-work commitments that you don't want to
compromise, or would you love lots of business travel
and high-powered meetings?

Common mistakes

✗ You bail out too early

Nothing in life is ever perfect, and it's tempting during a rough patch simply to blame your troubles on your job and go hunting for another one. However, financial considerations aside, it's always worth pausing to consider before you do this. What else may be making you feel dissatisfied? Is it someone or something that could be sorted out with a little patience and effort? Could it be that you're simply bored at the moment? If you *do* decide it's time to move on, make sure you've done your homework first so that your new role brings real benefits and you don't simply move from one unsatisfactory situation into another.

✗ You forget the importance of your own attitude

There's an old song that contains the line, 'If you can't be with the one you love, love the one you're with'. It may sound clichéd but it's a useful motto to bear in mind in the context of your job. If it would be difficult for you to leave your current working situation, your challenge is to discover its benefits rather than fretting about being stuck where you are. Quite often, contentment comes from the way you choose to perceive things. It might be an old-fashioned view, but counting your blessings—rather than cursing your luck—can make all the difference to how you feel about something!

STEPS TO SUCCESS

✔ Understand that job satisfaction results from many different elements, including having an interest in your work, utilising your strengths, and compatibility with your own values.

✔ Remember that your skills aren't the same as your strengths. Identify what you're interested in and what you do best, and look for areas where these come together.

✔ Talk to your boss—if he or she isn't making the most of your strengths, then it's best all round if something's done about it.

✔ Remember that there's more to a job than just being good at it or earning a suitable wage. Assess whether your working life is compatible with your personality and values.

✔ Keep in mind the context of your job. Rather than worry about being trapped, work out the benefits of your current situation and make the most of them.

Useful links

About.com, Human Resources:
http://humanresources.about.com
HR-Guide.Com:
www.hr-guide.com
HRM Guide:
www.hrmguide.co.uk
hrVillage.com:
www.hrvillage.com

Identifying your marketable skills

Most people tend to think too narrowly about their marketable skills, and as a result end up underselling themselves when they're looking for a promotion or a new job. If you're wondering whether to make a complete career change—or are just thinking about applying for a new job in the same industry—it'll help if you take a step-by-step approach to examining your life and work experiences. Then you'll be able to assess which of your skills are the most marketable.

There are two real benefits to thinking about your 'marketability'. The first, and most pragmatic, is that it'll help you to focus and to write a more powerful CV. The second is that it'll help you to present yourself more professionally to a potential employer. You'll feel confident about what you have to offer and will inevitably sell yourself better.

Step one: Begin with your main objective in mind

Before you start to identify your marketable skills, you need to know what kind of a position you're looking for. This will help you focus and put into context what skills you want to use in your next job.

First, consider the following questions:

- What are your personal and professional goals?
- What educational, work, and leisure experiences have you got under your belt that will help you reach your goals?
- Do you have a realistic picture of the match between your skills and your career goal?

If you're planning on changing careers, it's important to realise that you may have many transferable skills that will be marketable in a new position. Or you may have skills that you haven't used for some time that you could resurrect in a different type of employment.

It takes a lot of time and energy to identify your marketable skills. And although it's not an easy task, it's one of the most important you can undertake because it helps you to plan your job campaign and to target the best potential employers. It should also give you a confidence boost about what you have to offer.

Step two: Write a brief life/work biography

Take time to sit down and write a 3–5 page history of your life that includes significant events when you were growing up, important educational achievements, and a summary of your work experiences. As you write about each of these, describe what you liked and what you didn't like, and what you accomplished. What were you most proud of? Also, describe what you did during times when you weren't working, and how you felt about those activities. Make sure that there are at least seven key events in your biography.

Now ask yourself what, if anything, did writing your biography tell you about potential marketable skills that you might have? Be as honest as you can about the following:

I Educational assessment

Whether or not you included much detail on your educational experiences, these questions will help you make a useful assessment so you can highlight your main skills and interests:

- Which teachers did you like best and why?
- Which teachers did you like least and why?
- Which subjects did you like best and why?
- Which subjects did you like least and why?
- Which subjects did you get the best marks in and why?
- Which subjects did you get the worst marks in and why?

Based on what you've written, identify five key skills or knowledge areas that you might like to use in your next position.

2 Work-experience assessment

Review each of the jobs that you've held and ask yourself the following questions:

- What was my favourite job and why?
- What was my least favourite job and why?
- Which of these jobs would I do even if I didn't get paid? Why?
- Which jobs really challenged me and helped me to develop personally and professionally? Why?

As before, based on what you've written, identify five key skills or knowledge areas that you might like to use in your next position.

3 Leisure-activity assessment

In the times you're not working (whether evenings and weekends, or longer periods of time when perhaps you've been between jobs), what do you really enjoy doing with your leisure time? Here are questions to consider:

- What skills have you developed from a hobby that might be marketable?
- What skills have you developed from your travels?
- What skills have you developed from other leisure-time activities?

■ Is there something you do for fun that you always
dreamed of getting paid for?

Again, identify the five most marketable skills you have from
your leisure-activity assessment.

Now go over what you've written and create a list of at
least 10 major achievements in your life. Don't worry about
whether or not they're work-related. When you've
completed this list, rank your achievements in order, with
number one being your most important achievement,
number two being your second most important
achievement, and so on.

Step three: Compile a skills inventory

Once you've assessed your major achievements, the next
step is to create a final skills inventory by going over
everything that you've listed so far and grouping your skills
into the following categories:

■ **management skills.** Make a list of all your skills that
are related to management in any way. Although your
current job title may not classify you as 'a manager',
you may still do some activities that are considered
managerial. These can include policy formulation, policy
implementation, conducting performance reviews,
hiring, firing, project responsibilities, problem solving,
budgetary responsibilities, planning, organising,
presenting, and so on.

- **training skills.** Now list all your training skills, including any informal training you may have done. Training can be for individuals or for groups. Also list any qualifications you may have received for courses that you're certified to teach. Include any other professional training courses, seminars, and symposiums you've attended.

- **documentation-related skills** List all your documentation-related skills where you've prepared reports, manuals, summarised research, conducted studies, and so on.

- **technical skills.** Note down all your technical skills — these may include operating machines or computers, any specialised knowledge, any manufacturing, sales, engineering, personnel, or other skills that haven't been mentioned in any of the categories above.

- **interpersonal skills.** Make a list of all your interpersonal skills. Although they're harder to define, these skills can 'make or break' an application for a new position. This list could include any of the following skills: communication, facilitation (i.e. making things happen), mentoring, conciliation, negotiation, team building, and so on.

- **other skills.** Create a category of 'other skills' for any of your qualities, attributes or experiences that don't fit into the above categories. Often, these skills are something unique that you have to offer, making you more attractive, and giving you the edge over other candidates.

Step four: Compare your skills inventory with your career goals

By now, you should have quite a long list of potentially marketable skills. Go back through this list and tick or highlight the skills that most closely match your career goals. From your highlighted list, choose the 10 skills that you think are most marketable. Ask yourself, 'If I were recruiting someone for this job, are these the skills I'd be looking for?'. If you're lacking any essential skills for the job you really want, you should obviously make plans to acquire these as soon as you can.

Take each of the top 10 skills you've listed and write a sentence describing how you've actively put this skill into practice. For example: 'Used conciliation skills to solve a major problem between production and sales'. Or 'Conducted quality training in the finance department, leading to a 15% decrease in invoicing errors'.

Step five: Do a reality test and review your skills

Through your networking, identify someone who's doing the job that you'd really like to have. Ask him or her to review your list of skills and see whether they agree that your skills are a match for this kind of position. If they don't think there's a match, ask him or her what skills you need to gain.

Alternatively, you could ask what kind of a job would be a better match for someone with your skills. Another reality check is to ask those closest to you to review your skills and to see whether you've accidentally left anything out.

Finally, you can now turn your list of marketable skills into valuable information in your covering letter (if you include one) for any job application, and on your CV.

Common Mistakes

✗ **You skip this process and jump into writing your CV**

You may think that you already know all your skills, but identifying your marketable skills always produces some surprising and creative results that will help you market yourself better. Sometimes, it even helps you to see that you may have chosen the wrong job objective, and then you're able to alter your career goals to exploit all that you have to offer more fully.

✗ **You discount early life experiences**

You think to yourself, 'It doesn't matter what I did at school or in my first job. That was so long ago'. But often there are clues to your strongest skills and to your life's purpose in these early experiences.

✗ You're unrealistic about the match between your skills and your career goal

You may want to change from a job in information systems to a job in personnel, but if you haven't had any specialised training or experience in the new area, you won't be able to make the leap. Make sure that you do the reality test before you actually start your job search.

STEPS TO SUCCESS

✔ Decide on your objectives and your career goal. What do you want to achieve in your next job?

✔ List all your life skills and experiences—from what you achieved at school to every aspect of the jobs that you've done so far. Don't leave out anything—include any sporting triumphs, for example—and be honest with yourself.

✔ Draw up a master list of your skills grouping them into the following categories: management, training, documentation, technical, interpersonal—and anything else left over. You'll be surprised at how many marketable skills you have when looked at like this!

✔ Compare your skills with what you need to achieve your career goal. Ask others whether they think you've got the right skills (and make plans to fill any gaps if necessary). Then write your CV and apply for the next job that appeals to you.

Useful link

Monster:
www.monster.co.uk

Deciding to take a risky career move

Everything in business today is risky, and there's no such thing as a safe bet. It's certainly risky to leave a familiar job with routines, expectations, and objectives that you're comfortable with to test the limits of your courage and skills in a strange environment. But, as thousands of redundant employees in global companies can attest, it's not exactly safe holding on to a job that's as dependable as a leaky lifeboat. Whether you should decide to make that risky career move is entirely up to the nature of the risk and your ability to cope with the possible negative consequences.

The risk itself may be made up of any number of factors, such as your ability to move into an unfamiliar job or your ability to move into an unfamiliar organisation. Are you jumping from a traditional industry to a newer one? Or are you leaping back into the 'Old Economy' world after trying your luck in a hi-tech, high-pressure, go-go 'New Economy' environment? Are you considering leaving a stable, secure position that's limited in its prospects in favour of the white-knuckle environment of a start-up?

Are you about to move from a solid public organisation into a family-owned business? Is the family that owns the business your own? These are just some of the questions you need to think about before you do anything drastic.

Step one: Identify what 'acceptable risk' means to you

Only you know the risks you're ready to take in terms of your career. If you're young and single, with no obligations other than to yourself, you can probably afford to take on a few risky moves. These high-profile actions can give you early boosts that could position you for more momentum-driven rewards later in your career. If you're older, perhaps with a family or other responsibilities, you may not be quite as willing to try your luck with a high-risk/high-reward venture, such as a start-up enterprise.

TOP TIP

If you feel uncomfortable in risky situations but still want to grow in your career, remember that there are no guarantees in today's marketplace, so taking steps to avoid taking a risk might actually be the worst thing you could do.

For some people, the notion of going into a shaky entrepreneurial environment after drawing a steady salary for years would be unthinkable. For others, depending on only one income source, as opposed to the multiple sources of revenue available to an entrepreneur, may make them feel vulnerable.

The following points are key questions to ask yourself while considering whether you should take the risk or not:

- Do the benefits outweigh the potential costs of the risk?
- How many people depend utterly on the regular income your current job provides?
- Is there a back-up plan in case your gamble fails?
- Is it possible to return to your original position if you decide that your experiment wasn't as rewarding as you'd hoped?

Step two: Know your goals

Make a list of your short- and long-term objectives. Read them through, and ask yourself whether your current position will help you achieve them. If your position is unlikely to help you get to where you want to be, can you make slight adjustments to your present job in order to position yourself better for achieving your dreams? Or do you think you need to leave your position entirely?

TOP TIP
Take your time! To make sure that you don't regret your ultimate decision, give yourself all the time you need to make your choice wisely and

---

**calmly. Think it through methodically, and then
take a decision. Whatever the outcome, try to
learn from the decision-making process in
some way.**

Step three: Know what you value

List your less-tangible values. Which of the options open to
you is most likely to help you express those values? Your
current job or a new opportunity? Does one opportunity
actually position you to behave in ways that are contrary to
those values?

Here's one way to appreciate what your values really are:
close your eyes and imagine yourself at a much older age,
looking back at your life. First, imagine that you've had a
really full and satisfying life. Take a sheet of paper and
write down the things that you're proud to have done. What
were the best bits, that give you joy to remember? Now
imagine that you're looking back over a wasted life. What
do you regret and what do you wish you had done more of?
For example, you might write along the following lines:

Time and energy well spent in a full and satisfying life

- Family: time spent talking, helping kids develop,
  enjoying being together, loving and being loved.
- Building solid friendships for love, sharing, support, and
  learning.

- Business: created something bigger than myself, developed good understanding of clients' needs, developed new ways to help.
- Helping others.
- Developing myself to understand others better.

In a wasted life I would regret:

- Not travelling and learning about other cultures.
- Wasting time on appearances rather than substance.
- Lost contacts with family and friends.
- Staying employed all my life for the 'security'.
- Wasting my creativity.
- Harming others or failing to help where help was needed and I was able.
- Poor health as a result of not looking after my body.

Your answers will help you to gain an idea of what you want out of life, and to highlight what is missing at the moment.

Step four: Conduct a risk/benefit analysis

This is the process that'll help you determine whether the potential reward outweighs the potential pain. There are several methods for analysing the potential costs, but the easiest is simply to create two columns. List the potential pain in one column and the potential gain or reward in the

other. The column that has the longer list is the one that
should receive serious consideration.

A variation of this method is to assign points (from 1 to 10,
for example) or potential monetary values to each item. You
can then either compare the grand totals or assess each
pain/reward item on its own merit.

Step five: Consider the people you'd be working with

Who do you have the most in common with? This isn't a
question of who you'd be most comfortable spending an
afternoon watching television or playing tennis with. Rather,
whose visions and ideals are most compatible with your
own? The opportunity to work with those who inspire,
support, and encourage you is an exciting one, and may
be something not to be missed.

Common mistakes

✗ **You make the wrong choice**
As there are no guarantees, there's always a chance
that you'll make the wrong choice—or at least
the choice that feels wrong to you as you begin to
experience 'buyer's remorse'. Have faith in your
risk-assessment strategy, and carefully watch how that

risk plays itself out. There's always something positive to be gained from every adventure.

✗ You don't make any choice at all

Contradictory as it may sound, making no choice is still making a choice. And this is the one that's almost guaranteed to net you no gain at all. Modern business is full of risky moves. Those who relish the thrill of the risk, shift, and change will be the ones who will ultimately benefit from the growth and added self-awareness that comes from the adventure of being engaged in contemporary commerce.

STEPS TO SUCCESS

✔ Take time over your decision-making—it needs careful planning and thoughtful consideration of your options.

✔ 'Acceptable risk' varies from person to person. Identify how far you're able or willing to go.

✔ Decide on certain goals and assess whether or not your current position can help you achieve these.

✔ Think about what's necessary in a job in order to bring fulfilment to your life.

✔ Remember that any risk can result in a loss—so never risk more than you are willing/able to lose. There are no guarantees, but on a positive note, benefits can be gained from most experiences.

Useful links

Executive Action International:
www.executive-action.co.uk
'How to Bounce Back From Setbacks', Fast Company:
www.fastcompany.com/online/45/bounceback.html
Monster:
www.monster.co.uk

Looking for a new challenge

If you're feeling dissatisfied with your job, or your life in general, it may be that you're simply looking for a new challenge. If this sounds like you, you're not alone! Today, adults are increasingly displaying what are traditionally 'childlike' tendencies. In fact, in our entertainment-on-demand culture, we're becoming increasingly fickle and our attention spans are becoming shorter. The problem is that, the more we come to expect instant gratification—finding the perfect job, for instance—the more likely it is that we'll become dissatisfied with what we've got. After a while, you'll probably end up yearning for something more meaningful, something unique, that represents your individuality and value as a human being.

So how can you find a new challenge in this rich mix of possibilities and opportunities: one that will reflect your individuality, keep you interested, and satisfy your long-term needs? This chapter will invite you to question your beliefs and desires, and will point you in the right direction.

Step one: Consider some common predicaments

I want to find a new challenge but where should I start?

Remember that finding a new challenge isn't something that can be taken lightly or done in haste; it needs careful consideration and clarity of thought. Before anything else, you'll find it useful to hear yourself explain your feelings, and to hear someone else's view. Try talking things through with a trusted friend, mentor, or coach. If they ask the right questions, challenge any assumptions, and correct any misapprehensions you should be able to see your way more clearly.

Think about what's happening now. Maybe you've reached a natural transition point in your life. It may be that an event or series of events has caused you to re-evaluate your situation. Work out what's prompted you to start looking for a new challenge. Are office politics making your life at work tricky, or is it something in your personal life? Maybe your partner has changed jobs, or your kids have left home. It could be anything! At least if you know what's prompted this desire for a change you'll have some certainty—even if you don't yet know what to do next.

I've made the change to something that I've always wanted to do but am _still_ feeling dissatisfied! What's wrong with me?

Change is always disorientating, no matter how positive the change is on paper. You'll need time to adjust to your new surroundings, colleagues, and schedule, and to establish yourself in your new field. As a general guide, it can often take six months or more before someone feels comfortable with a new role. Think back to your previous position and remind yourself why you made the change. Refocus on your goals, and you should rediscover your momentum.

There's so much I want to do! How can I work out the best route?

Brainstorm! Write down what you want from your new challenge, then list all your ideas for potential challenges. By finding common themes, you'll be able to eliminate marginal ideas and focus on the challenge that meets the most criteria. Some of your ideas may not be right for you yet, but they may be in the future. Keep your list and refer back to it when you're ready for your *next* challenge!

I'm bored and frustrated, but don't want to take too much of a risk. How can I find a new challenge without losing my security?

Maybe it's not a career change you're looking for, but simply a new dimension in your life. Even small changes can make a vast difference to your state of mind, so find something that you can do *as well as* your current job. You might like to take up a sport, join a choir, or do some voluntary work. Once you find something that you're passionate about, it'll be easy to fit it into your schedule.

Step two: Know your values

If you're bored or frustrated, you're more likely to rush into doing something that you'll later regret. Before making any decisions, get to know yourself better. Take a look at your values and motivations, and work out what makes you feel happy and fulfilled. What do you want to achieve from this new challenge? What assumptions are you making? How would you like to feel once you've taken on the challenge? Do you have an end point in mind?

By looking at your motivations in this way—and by talking them through with an impartial confidant(e)—you'll be less likely to make a hasty mistake. Once you've taken on the challenge, you'll be more able to judge whether it's giving you what you wanted from it, or whether you need to rethink your approach.

Step three: Make a note of your good and bad experiences

Make a list of your best and worst times, and think about what made them such positive or negative experiences. This will help you to work out what ingredients your new challenge will need, and what should be avoided. If your current situation is one of your bad times, be especially careful when deciding what to do; you need to improve your situation, but you mustn't make any decisions out of desperation. If, on the other hand, your new challenge is an extension of a good time, that's great! It means that you're not being complacent; you're channelling the energy created by your positive experiences into even more positive outcomes.

Step four: Decide what you want from your new challenge

If you're clear about what you want to achieve in the longer term, you're more likely to set specific goals, make more informed choices, and put together a clearer plan. To help you to work out your motivations, ask yourself the questions below.

- **Do I want to learn something new?** If you want to stretch yourself intellectually and/or build expertise in a new area, you could consider doing an evening course, studying part-time, furthering your education in a more formal way (by studying for a qualification, for example), or stretching your mind with a more philosophical course of study.

- **Do I want to develop a new skill?** If you want to build on your practical skills you could do a weekend course, evening classes, or take some time off work to do a more intensive course. Do you know anyone with the skills you're interested in learning? Talk to them about the best way of learning.

- **Do I want to experience a new culture?** One way of refreshing your world view is to travel and take a job overseas. Travel helps people to see the world from other people's points of view, to witness how other cultures live, to explore new belief systems, and to push your boundaries of experience. One way of doing this in a constructive way is to travel with a voluntary organisation, such as Voluntary Service Overseas (VSO).

- **Do I want to meet new people?** Maybe you want to make new friends, or to broaden your circle of professional contacts. Involvement in new groups can bring many new opportunities and a fresh outlook.

Step five: Find advisers

Once you've narrowed your list of options, you can start to examine them more closely and work out which are better for you. Speak to friends, family, and mentors; you may find that they've got a clearer view of your motivations and capabilities than you have yourself!

Another way in which your network can help you is by providing inspiration. Is anyone you know doing anything which inspires or attracts you? You may not want to do exactly what they're doing, but it could give you some ideas or point you in the direction you want to take. Have a look at public figures, too: who do you consider particularly admirable or inspirational? What are they doing that attracts you?

Step six: Simplify your decision making

Don't overcomplicate things! Once you've identified your end goal, keep that in mind and everything else should fall into place around it. Ask yourself what needs to happen in order for your decision to be a success, and work out how to achieve this. You may need to ask for support or resources from a friend, colleague, or manager; it may be that, in order to fulfil your goal, you need some time away from work, with a guaranteed job to come back to.

Remember to try things out before you make any irrevocable decisions; always dip your toe in the water *before* taking the plunge! Carrying out research is not just a paper exercise; it should also be experiential.

Don't forget to have a 'Plan B' up your sleeve. Your plans may not work out, so—especially if you're making a complete break from what you're used to—you need to know what to do to retrieve the situation. This isn't a negative move; knowing that you have a back-up plan in place will enable you to throw yourself wholeheartedly into your new challenge.

Common mistakes

✗ **You don't think through all the options**
If you're feeling bored or frustrated, you could end up making a radical change in your life without thinking it through properly. Such hasty decisions may mean that you fail to achieve what you're hoping for, and make you regret what you've done. Whatever you decide, always have a back-up plan.

✗ **You make a series of bad decisions**
If the worst comes to the worst and you realise you've made a hasty decision, you might change direction rapidly, as you try to retrieve the situation—and your dignity—with the result that things go from bad to worse! Making one ill-thought-through decision on top of another will only compound the problem; instead you must pull back, admit your mistake, take stock, analyse where you've gone wrong, and start again.

✗ **You base your decision on a wrong premise**
Making a choice based on an emotional response to a situation is ill advised, as your analysis will be clouded by your emotions, and you may be trying to fix something that isn't the actual problem. Although you need to be emotionally in step with your decision, it should also have a firm base in reality. To ensure that

you've assessed the situation rationally, talk things through with a trusted confidant(e), asking them to question you, and play devil's advocate.

STEPS TO SUCCESS

✔ If you're feeling dissatisfied, ask yourself why. What do you really want to do? And what do you hope to achieve?

✔ Think about what additional courses you could attend, or what skills you could acquire outside your current job. Don't let yourself be shackled by imaginary boundaries.

✔ Ask friends, family, and mentors for their views on your proposed change of direction. They probably know you better than you imagine, and will be able to offer useful suggestions on your next step forward.

Useful links

About.com, Career Planning:
http://careerplanning.about.com
Alliance for Conflict Transformation:
www.tinyurl.com/2clwz4
CarersUK, Finding New Challenges:
www.carersuk.org/Information/Caringandbereavement/
Findingnewchallenges

The City and Guilds Institute:

www.city-and-guilds.co.uk

Cross Cultural Solutions:

www.tinyurl.com/2gs46y

Simple Laws for Making Good Decisions:

http://bottomlinesecrets.com/blpnet/article.html?
article_id=27567

Voluntary Services Overseas (VSO):

www.vso.org.uk

5
Researching the job market

Once you've decided that you really want to change your career direction, you'll obviously start to think about what type of job could be right for the new you. But when you start your job search, you need to have several different kinds of information. You'll need to research industry trends, find out details about the particular companies you're aiming for, and perhaps even do some research on the human resources manager of the company you think you might want to work for.

You'll want to keep in mind questions such as the following:

- What do I need to know about the industry I want to work in, that will help me to ask and answer intelligent questions?

- Where can I find out more information about the companies I've selected?

- What kind of information do I want to know about each of these companies?

■ **What would I like to know about the company (or companies) that I really want to work for so that I stand a better chance of writing a fantastic covering letter and then get an interview?**

Step one: Do the necessary groundwork

You may wonder why you have to research the job market and think that it's enough simply to scan the job adverts in the newspapers. But only a small percentage of people find jobs that they love through these ads. If you research the job market thoroughly, you'll have a clearer idea of what you're attracted to. You'll also be able to design your CV and covering letter more effectively and more intelligently when you've gathered useful background information.

Researching industry trends will help you to decide whether or not you want to stay in the industry you originally chose, or whether you really want to move to something entirely new. If the trends show that you're in a declining industry, it may be time for a change. Remember, too, that when you have an interview, it'll help you to ask informed questions (which always impresses personnel officers), and will help you to answer questions from a richer perspective.

How much time you spend on this initial research depends, of course, on the level of the job you're seeking. If you're hoping to land a high-level executive position in the same industry, you may already know most of the required information. But if you're seeking a high-level position in a new industry, you may need to spend several weeks on your job market research. If you're looking for a specialised position, you may not need to know as much about industry trends, but you'll want to do several days' research on your chosen organisations.

Step two: Start broadly and then narrow down your research

In the early stages of your research, you'll begin by researching industry trends. The main things you'll be looking for are:

- the major growth areas
- the major players
- the major challenges and problems for this industry

The first step in doing this research is to visit your nearest city or university library. Ask the reference librarian for help in finding reference guides and publications containing information about industry trends.

If you're not sure which industry you want work in, there are several good references and reports on attractive jobs and desirable companies. The *Financial Times* website **www.ft.com/companies** provides very valuable information on this topic, as does the UK Trade & Investment website (**www.uktradeinvest.gov.uk**) which has well-organised information about trends in various business sectors. *The Economist* website is another useful resource, providing business briefings by country (**www.economist.com/ countries**). In addition to these resources, some of the top business schools have websites that give good guidance on where to go and which directories to look at.

Step three: Research your chosen companies

The next step is to narrow your research by gathering information about the specific companies that you're aiming for in your job search. The key facts that you'll probably want to know about for each of these organisations are:

- size of the organisation (sales, profits, market share, numbers of employees)
- strong and weak points
- key competitors
- organisational culture
- how the company is organised
- key strategic challenges

Much of this information is now easily available on the Internet, which will save you a lot of time. Once you've found an organisation that you're interested in, get hold of a copy of their annual report. You'll probably be able to find this on their website, or if not, simply phone the company and ask them to send you a copy.

If you've chosen a local company, find ways to talk to employees about what it's like to work there and what its strengths and weaknesses are. You can also ask them about competitors, and about the key strategic challenges that the company is facing. If you don't know anyone who works there, you might consider attending local business meetings such as the Chamber of Commerce meetings, or other professional gatherings.

Several 'best company' websites are listed at the end of this chapter that will provide information about good companies to select, if you're not sure where to start.

Step four: Research information about a specific job

The things you'll typically want to know when you're looking for a specific job in a specific company are as follows:

- What would my tasks and responsibilities be?
- What qualifications are needed? What is the typical salary for a job like this?
- What can I find out about the human resources manager?

Most of these questions will be answered when you're at the interview, but if you can gather information about them ahead of time, you're better prepared for your covering letter, your CV, and your interview. If you found out about the job through an advertisement, then the tasks and responsibilities have probably been spelled out. On the other hand, if you haven't seen an advertisement but you know for sure that there's a job opening, phone and ask the company to send you a copy of the job description.

You'll want to find out as much as you can about the human resources manager, and you may be able to do this through business reference books, if he or she is at a high enough level. You can also do an Internet search to see if he or she has been mentioned in any publications, or has written any publications in your field. Professional associations may have information on this person if he or she is active in your professional field. And if you know other people in the company, you can use your contacts to find out as much as possible about the human resources manager, before you contact him or her. You're looking for any information that shows that you may have something in common. This is valuable information for your covering letter that you send to accompany your job application, and also strengthens relationship-building when you're being interviewed.

Common mistakes

✗ Your research isn't thorough enough
   If you don't do enough research about the industry, the company, and the job, you may say or do something

that shows your ignorance and jeopardises your chances. If you can demonstrate that you've done your homework, you'll really stand out from the crowd, and will have a better chance of being taken on.

✗ You do so much research that you can't keep track of it all

It's helpful to create files for each of the industries and companies that you're researching. Set up a filing system for all your information so that you can find what you need quickly. This is especially important when you're preparing for an interview. You might want to prepare a set of index cards listing key points that you want to remember. Carry these cards with you wherever you go to help you learn and remember important information.

STEPS TO SUCCESS

✔ Do your groundwork and decide what type of job really appeals to you.

✔ Work on your CV to make sure that it suits each job application.

✔ Spend time researching the various companies you think you might want to work for. Look at their websites and compare their expectations with what you think you can fulfil.

Useful links

Worktrain:

www.worktrain.gov.uk

Job Search:

www.jobsearch.co.uk

Jobs-by-email:

www.jobsite.co.uk

Sunday Times Best 100 Companies to Work For:

**www.timesonline.co.uk/tol/life_and_style/career_and_
jobs/best_100_companies**

6

Finding and working with search organisations

When you begin the job-search process, it's common to feel haunted by the so-called 'hidden job market'—that exclusive network that links the favoured few with the very best job opportunities. There are legitimate reasons for feeling like this, especially if you're trying to get started in a brand new type of job. Only a small percentage of open jobs are publicly announced. The very best jobs usually require a special set of skills or background, and companies use refined recruitment techniques to attract candidates for such unique positions.

One of those techniques is to retain a search organisation that specialises in ferreting out the best candidates for the open position. The trouble is that it's not easy to know about, much less apply for, these particular opportunities. And, among the very best search organisations, the general message to the public is: 'Don't find us. We'll find you'. Indeed, if individuals reach out to search organisations, the mere fact that they've done so almost automatically renders

them undesirable in the eyes of many of these companies. Just as banks only like to lend money to people who don't really need it, search organisations like to recruit candidates who aren't really looking for jobs.

With that closed-club impression, it's natural to feel as though actively setting out to attract the attention of search organisations is probably counter-productive. However, there are ways to use the connections and power of search organisations to promote your own career. This chapter will show you how.

Step one: Ask yourself some basic questions

Before you do anything, remember that you should never pay a search organisation. The client is the recruiting company. Search organisations receive their fees from the company, valued at roughly 30% of the new employee's first year's salary. But you need to consider the following points if you're thinking about looking for your next job with the help of one or more search organisations:

- Do you really need a search organisation to help you find your next job?
- How quickly do you need a new job?

■ Should you work with a contingency organisation or a retained search organisation?

The difference between contingency search organisations and retained search organisations

A contingency search organisation only makes its money when it successfully places a candidate. Contingency organisations usually fill junior to middle-level executive positions, with salaries ranging from £35,000 to £100,000. A retained search organisation works with more senior positions, receiving its fee regardless of whether certain positions are successfully filled. Both are legitimate forms of business; however, it's generally agreed that retained search organisations have a higher-quality relationship with their client company—a long-term interest in which the mutual goal is the company's prosperity. With a contingency search organisation, the emphasis is more likely to be on the individual placement. So both you and the recruiting company could find yourselves in a wrong match.

In most cases, there's nothing wrong with working with more than one search organisation at the same time. You're the one in charge of your own future! So do seriously reconsider signing with a search organisation that insists on an exclusive contract with you. Don't forget that because you're not the paying client, your own personal interests won't be part of the organisation's business concerns. Therefore, you should be able to market and represent yourself freely elsewhere.

Step two: Identify the best search organisations for the type of position you're seeking

Use word of mouth and other indirect marketing techniques for identifying the best search organisations and helping them find you. Ask your friends, colleagues, and college career centres to introduce you to the services they've found to be satisfactory. Go where search organisation consultants go. Attend high-profile business receptions, and human resource seminars in your community or industry. Participate as a speaker (or even a volunteer) at business symposia. Write articles for your industry journal.

The best way to make contact with a search organisation is to phone a search organisation consultant specifically recommended to you by a friend or colleague. Make sure you've got an expertly prepared CV ready to send immediately. If you don't have a personal introduction, send the CV with a covering letter describing your overall credentials and abilities.

Step three: Be prepared

You may be invited to come in for an interview at very short notice. Or you may be notified that your CV has been keyed into the organisation's database. Assuming that your CV

CHANGE CAREERS SUCCESSFULLY

contains the important keywords associated with your career path, your information will then come up the next time a suitable position is researched. Working with search companies is likely to be a long-term proposition, where both you and the consultant will find success if and when a compatible opening is available at a client company.

If you're contacted by a search organisation that you're unfamiliar with, check that the organisation's going to be able to fulfil your needs. It's a good idead to ask them who their client companies have been. Any organisation that you would want to work with will freely offer a shortlist of prestigious client companies.

Step four: Choose your search organisations selectively

While you should never succumb to the pressure of signing an exclusive deal with only one organisation, you also should sign with only a small number of organisations, so you can stay focused and in control of your schedule of interviews.

After the initial interview with the recruiting company, follow up with that company in the standard ways, such as sending a thank-you letter. Search organisations shouldn't try to stand in the way of the relationship you cultivate with the recruiting company. The successful recruitment will benefit all three parties, and it continues to be up to you to do your part to improve the chances of receiving an offer.

Step five: Listen to feedback

If you find that you haven't landed that perfect job, despite a number of interviews, listen to any feedback you get from the search organisation. Their consultant may see you as the best possible candidate for an ideal position; however, there may be a small element in your personal demeanour, grooming, or body language that is spoiling your chances. If the consultant suggests anything that might improve your chances, and it doesn't require a fundamental shift in your basic nature or values, seriously consider following the advice you're given.

Common mistakes

✗ You waste your time with low-quality consultants and search organisations

Insist on a personal meeting at their offices. If they then tell you, in return, that they'd prefer a telephone relationship, or if you find that their offices are shabby, these are excellent indicators that their clients will probably not be top-market employment opportunities for you.

✗ You wait until you need to find a new job before cultivating a relationship with a search-organisation consultant

Some of the most successful search organisations receive up to 300 CVs a day, so you have to compete for their attention. Additionally, there may not be any openings for positions that you're best qualified for. As new job opportunities are rare, you need to be in the search organisation's system long before you're desperate for a new job.

✗ You try to camouflage an irregular career path with clever answers

Most consultants and recruiting managers have heard the language typically used to camouflage a firing or a dismissal for a company's downsizing. If you're only available now because you were dismissed or fired, be as candid as possible.

STEPS TO SUCCESS

✔ Do your market research. Decide which search organisations would be good to work with. Then find a way to get on to their books.

✔ Be prepared. Make sure your CV is up to date and looks professional before you contact the organisation. Just in case they want to see you immediately. Similarly, make sure your 'interview clothes' are clean, pressed and ready!

✔ Stay in touch with your search organisation consultant. If you accept a new job, and if you've achieved a mutually satisfactory relationship with your search-organisation consultant, stay in touch. Send them excellent candidates for other positions that may become available. Meet for lunch now and then. You don't have to make that person your best friend. But the days of working for one company for the rest of your life are over. The chances are that you'll be searching for a new position within a few years. Use that earlier relationship to keep moving forward along your career path towards your future.

Useful links

Global Executive:
www.economist.com/business/globalexecutive/
Executive Grapevine:
www.askgrapevine.com

7 Creating and balancing a portfolio career

Job satisfaction takes many forms. For some people, it means a relatively secure income; for others, it's the opportunity to concentrate on a single, fascinating career. Then there are those for whom job satisfaction comes from having a variety of different careers (either all at once or consecutively) that allows them to earn a livelihood exploring lots of different interests.

To critical observers, this approach to career development — known as the 'portfolio career — may appear unfocused and directionless. However, it's an excellent way for you to enjoy different opportunities and life experiences (sights, friends, and so on) in today's fast-moving world. And because the so-called 'job for life' is virtually extinct, the single most compelling argument for suppressing curiosity in favour of the illusion of job security no longer exists.

In fact, portfolio-career practitioners discover that their multiple sources of income provide them with a more secure feeling than depending on the continuing goodwill and loyalty of a single income source. And, even though you're self-employed and indulging your passions and spirit of adventure, that doesn't necessarily mean that you'll incur financial penalties. With multiple sources of income, you may even find that you make more money than you would in a traditional career.

Step one: Assess your personal qualities

If you're considering ways to build a portfolio career, it'll help if you first ask yourself some key questions to check whether this really is the best course of action for you:

- How high is your tolerance for uncertainty and insecurity?
- Are you self-motivated?
- Do you relish change and meeting new people?
- Do you depend on the social life and intimacy that being a regular member of a single workplace gives you?

If you can cope with uncertainty, can answer 'yes' to the second and third questions, and can manage without being part of a corporate environment, then you've passed the first hurdle.

TOP TIP

If you're ever between jobs and your industry is in a recession, you can use the portfolio-career concept to improve your marketability when you're back on the job market. Take a strategic

---

approach to designing your portfolio career. Make sure that each assignment you accept gives you additional information, experience, or exposure to key players in your industry. The more varied your experience within a single industry, the better your understanding is of important trends in that industry. So, you'll be better qualified for strategic positions later. Industry experts who've got a bird's-eye view are often in a better position to command higher salaries.

Step two: Remember that you don't have to leave your job straight away

You can start to create a portfolio career even when you've got a full-time job. In fact, your full-time job could be the keystone to your portfolio career as you build a lifelong CV of ever-increasing experience, responsibility, and variety. Or you can build a portfolio career as a sideline, using your spare time and energy to develop passions that are either related or entirely disconnected from your full-time work.

Creating a portfolio career is more a matter of perspective and approach than needing to have the courage to 'go public' with an all-or-nothing announcement that you're now a fully committed self-employed individual. While portfolio careers often entail at least one independent source of income, they don't require that you abandon a full-time source of financial security.

If you talk about your plans for building your portfolio career with others, you need to make sure they get the right impression. An overall sense of purpose and big-picture direction is what separates you from idle dabblers. You can potter and experiment to your heart's content, but when you talk about your work, or even think about it in the privacy of your own mind, always regard your portfolio career as a unified whole, rather than as a simple collection of 'odd jobs'.

Step three: Explore the big-picture view of your career

Your big-picture approach to your portfolio career will probably evolve over time, but you need at least to start out with a general idea of what the big picture will look like once you've put all your job puzzle pieces together. Just as a collector gathers items according to some kind of theme, so a portfolio career also requires that, ultimately, your varied experience will contribute to some sort of unified result. Ask yourself, 'What do I want myself to be all about?' and keep that question at the centre of your mind as your career progresses and jobs accumulate.

To give yourself the best chance of success at each of your portfolio jobs, always be businesslike to the extent that's appropriate to your job. Make a point of reading any relevant industry publications and books, so you can keep up with trends and speak knowledgeably of the strategic issues facing your industry.

Step four: Market yourself as if you were a management consultant

Socialise, and volunteer to help out in any situations that are likely to put you in front of leaders of industry and key decision-makers. Other useful things you can do include the following:

- Participate in local industry groups and contribute as much as you can.
- Eliminate drains on your time whenever possible. Unnecessary hours spent in front of the TV or reading may prove to be time-expensive luxuries that you can no longer afford.
- Learn to say 'no'. You'll have to learn to balance the temptations of pursuing exciting opportunities with staying focused on your overall career theme.
- And learn to say 'yes'. You may meet an important person or learn a new skill that will make the doors to other opportunities swing wide open.

Step five: Keep a journal and have fun!

Some career paths seem to be more like career trenches. You may not see exactly where they're leading you. By keeping a journal, you'll be creating a map for retrospective analysis, and when you take time to look back, you'll be able to see the bigger picture and the overall purpose of your journey.

You may be the only person you know who's following an unusual, zigzag pattern of career progression. And you may be alone in your values and the choices you make. There could be high costs in choosing this kind of work style. But there's one reward that you have total control over: the ability to enjoy the process. There'll be benefits that are available to you only if you have a sense of independence, which often comes with knowing you've got an alternative source of income; the ability to pick and choose your assignments; the chance to live in beautiful parts of the world; the opportunity to travel, if you wish; and the chance to move freely through corporate hierarchies, and meet exciting and powerful people at all levels of organisations.

Common mistakes

✗ You become strapped for cash
Start this adventure with a cushion of six months' living expenses, if you can. Additionally, follow the practices of management consultants whenever possible: they sell their services by the value of results (not by tasks or time) and they insist on at least 50% in advance of the work.

✗ You become bogged down
It's possible to become overloaded. It's hard to turn down work, especially when you're unsure where and

when the next opportunity will come, but overloading yourself robs you of the benefits of this kind of lifestyle and work style. It is important for the sake of your own mental and physical health to take time off and get plenty of exercise and rest.

✗ You become isolated

Employees who work full-time in a congenial work environment have the advantage of everyday camaraderie, companionship, and creative synergy. As a portfolio careerist, it's very important to make sure your business and social networks are current and thriving. You must have friends you can turn to either so you can share ideas with them or simply so you've got someone to relax with.

✗ Your skills become out of date

If you were working full time for a company, you may have enjoyed training and development benefits. As a portfolio careerist, you may be fully self-employed. It's up to you to make sure your skills are current and marketable, and you may be the one who must pay for the necessary training courses or schemes.

STEPS TO SUCCESS

✔ Make sure you've got the right character for a portfolio career: it isn't the right answer for everyone, and in fact it's best avoided if you don't like working alone or feel scared of new challenges.

✔ Don't take financial risks. Try to have a financial cushion of at least half a year's salary to keep you going through leaner times.

✔ Keep focused. Take every opportunity you can to promote yourself and mingle with people who could make a difference to the next stage of your career. This is your chance to be noticed and blow your own trumpet!

Useful link

Portfolio Career:
www.creativekeys.net/portfoliocareer3.htm

Moving sideways: Benefiting from a lateral move

As mentioned in earlier chapters, the whole notion of a 'job for life' has vanished these days. To make a success of your career now, you need more creativity, flexibility, and originality than ever before. The good news is that the rigid assumption that there's only one way to succeed in a company—that is, by promotion—has also vanished. Not so long ago, if you weren't moving up, you were almost certainly fast-tracked out the door.

But today both employers and employees are discovering that lateral career moves are a creative way to build exciting companies and rewarding futures. For their part, individuals recognise that the more varied their skill sets and experiences, the more value they can bring to their employers. This translates into increased marketability, as well as additional job security in changing times, and if you're looking for a new challenge without necessarily wanting a new employer, it could be an excellent opportunity for you.

If you're willing to move laterally, you may protect yourself from being laid off as your company downsizes in one department while expanding operations in other, more profitable divisions. Employers, by contrast, are coming to recognise that lateral moves are a way of retaining valuable employees (as well as protecting themselves from losing valued talent to their competitors). Top talent is difficult and expensive to identify, recruit, and retain. Top talent is also hungriest for new challenges and growth opportunities and will be quick to leave if not fed with them. Employers are beginning to understand that moving eager and interested employees within the organisation is an extremely valuable approach to employee development, and one which will serve them well in the future. This chapter will help you to consider whether a lateral, or sideways, move might be right for you.

Step one: Consider the implications of a sideways move

You might think that a lateral move will reflect negatively on you. But this isn't necessarily the case. As with almost every business decision, you get the best value if you make your choice for strategic reasons and then learn from the experience. You can make a lateral move for any number of reasons, and you may experience some surprising benefits in the process (understanding the ways other parts of the business are run, for example). Capture those benefits as added strategic value and you may actually boost your career prospects in the long run.

If you're toying with the idea of moving sideways within the organisation—perhaps, in certain circumstances, even down the ladder—then ask yourself the following key questions:

- If your company is downsizing, or if there are other elements in your life requiring more of your attention and energy, will a lateral move help you stay happily employed?
- Will a lateral move give you valuable on-the-job exposure to business functions that will help you to accelerate your upward mobility?
- How receptive is your employer to the principle of hiring from within and providing lateral experience in order to develop employees?
- Is there a monitoring system in place within the management so that your career path will be tracked and your new skills set will be expanded further later on?

Step two: Identify why you're exploring the option of a lateral move

You need to be sure that there's a genuine reason why a lateral move fits in with your chosen career path. Before you do anything rash, ask yourself why moving sideways might be best for you:

- Does the next logical upward step in your career path require certain experience that you don't yet have?
- Have you just finished a protracted period of high-pressure productivity and now need a lighter load for a short time?
- Are you taking demanding classes to increase your market value in the long run and need a less strenuous set of responsibilities during your workday?
- Are family pressures preventing you from keeping up a demanding travel schedule?
- Are you committed to the company in the long run and want to understand as much of it as you can? Or do you simply want some variety?

Once you've given honest answers to the above, you'll be in a much better to move forwards in a positive fashion.

Step three: Investigate internal employment policies

It's all very well deciding that you want to make a lateral move, but you need to find out whether your organisation has a policy in place that supports such scenarios. Talk to employees who've made that choice to discover whether their long-term career ambitions are still being protected.

You also need to seek out opportunities in areas in which your company is thriving or continuing to expand. You don't want to move to the department that's about to experience a major downsizing! Try to have a chat with other employees in those divisions to discover what the environment is like and whether senior management generally supports individual ambition and career development.

TOP TIP

Employers that support skills development and communication across the whole business are the most likely to back your aim to make a lateral move. After all, the best CEOs are the ones with the broadest exposure to the spectrum of corporate functions. However, if you observe that your company's most senior leaders have achieved their success via single channels of departmental experience, it might be better to stay on your current departmental ladder or change employers if your career plan involves wide variety.

Step four: Consider the desirability of the openings that are available

Before you even apply for a job that would be a sideways move, compare your current position with what you're thinking about moving to:

■ Would you have to take a pay cut?

- How long do you think you'd remain interested in that particular work?
- Does the new department show promise for continued growth and opportunity?
- Is the management team of your chosen department well received and respected among their own superiors?

You'll also find it helpful if you think about what you like best about your job as it stands and try to imagine whether you'll find the same elements in your prospective new assignment. How will you stay in touch with your current team members? Would you be able to return to your present assignment when and if you desire? If not, would that make an important difference to you?

Step five: Check your potential for success and failure in your possible new position

Work out roughly how long it will take to achieve your current level of proficiency (and salary, if appropriate) in your new assignment. Are the measures of success acceptable to you? Are the requirements for upward mobility on this new ladder attractive to you?

You also need to think about your prospects for development outside the company. Does this new ladder present opportunities for expanding your marketability in the external job market? Will it provide you with technical training and experiences to boost your competence, therefore rewarding you sufficiently for the risk you'd be taking now?

Step six: Plan for transitions

Once you've landed a lateral position, make sure that you and your new manager have worked out a plan to integrate you into the new team as smoothly as possible. You may have put a great deal of advance thought and work into making the transition, but your new co-workers might not be enthusiastic or ready to accept you as a new player.

Don't assume that just because you're a long-standing employee in the company, you're at home in this new division. If you're replacing a beloved former co-worker, you may run up against additional resistance to your new appointment. Do as much as you can to make yourself welcome in the group.

Common mistakes

✗ You choose a bad time to move
One of the worst things that can happen is if you decide to leave a secure position only to discover that your new job becomes a casualty of a downsizing exercise. Thoroughly investigate the prospects of your new assignment, just as you would if you were applying

for the job from the outside. Understand the roles that this particular position and the department play in the company's long-term plans. If you can't see how this work serves your employer's mission critical objectives, hold out for another opportunity.

✗ **You become unintentionally slow-tracked**
If you make a lateral move, especially if it's to reduce your stress load temporarily for a personal reason, you may find yourself accidentally on the list of expendable employees. Be sure to invest time regularly to market yourself to colleagues throughout the business. For example, go to key meetings on a regular basis or have lunch with your former manager to stay in touch with developments in your original department. Stay current with your company's developments and objectives, and position yourself to make another jump into a more critical job as soon as you can.

✗ **You make too many lateral moves with no apparent growth or progression**
Remember that, desirable as lateral moves may be, your career path must still show regular upward mobility. When you make lateral moves, try to take a job that pays in some way, even though it's on the same level in the organisational chart. Or take a lateral move to learn more management skills elsewhere, and then return to your original department at a higher rank.

Lateral career moves shouldn't be used routinely as a preventative measure against losing your job, or as a way to tread water for longer than during a very short downturn in the economy or your industry. Instead, you should use them as a valuable strategic career management tool and, when you're able to discuss your recent career path in those terms, you'll find that a lateral move can be an excellent springboard to an even better future.

STEPS TO SUCCESS

✔ Decide why you want to want to make a lateral move. Make sure that you're making the move for the right reasons, and that even if you're not gaining promotion, then you'll be learning new skills.

✔ Investigate potential new positions. Look at the structure of your own organisation and decide whether you'd be better off making a lateral move to another company or whether you should stay with the business you know. Take an objective view of your business and the divisions that are expanding and the most successful. Is there an opening that you might be able to apply for?

✔ Don't be afraid to reconsider. If the lateral move turns out not to be as wonderful as you were hoping for, and if after a while you feel there are no possibilities for promotion or expanding your skills, accept the fact that maybe it wasn't such a good idea after all, and start planning your next step up your career ladder. It's not the end of the world, and you'll have drawn many useful lessons from the whole experience.

Useful links

Monster.com:

http://wlb.monster.com/articles/lateralmoves

PersonnelToday.com:

www.personneltoday.com

Surviving the first week in a new job

If you decided to change career direction and have landed a great new role, congratulations! Starting in a new job can be daunting for anyone, regardless of experience or grade. The first week of a job can be especially difficult, when it is most important to try to make a good first impression and set a precedent for how you will manage your team.

Rather than viewing your first week as something difficult - something to be endured before you are a fully fledged member of the team - approach it positively. Seeing it as an opportunity to start things off as you mean to go on can go a long way to ensuring that you not only 'survive' your first week, but that you find it an enjoyable and satisfying experience.

There are a number of things that you can do to prepare for your first week in a new job and techniques explained in this chapter will ensure that you set some great foundations for your future at your new company.

Step one: Think about your strategy for these common questions

What should I do if I'm given tasks I don't feel ready for?

Even people going into their third or fourth job (never mind a brand new career direction) can find new roles challenging, and it's very likely that some elements of your new position will be new to you. Try not to panic too soon, however: be realistic and accept that you won't necessarily know how to do everything right away or know how the company works inside out. Ask for clarification when you need it rather than struggling on trying to keep your questions to yourself: your new colleagues will expect that you'll need some extra help in the early days. In fact, showing that you realise you need to tap into their knowledge of the company is a great way of building good relationships and showing your colleagues that you value their experience. If you've moved into a management role, having this type of contact with your new team will also help you work out which of your staff may need careful handling (if they appear rude, aggressive, or indifferent, say), and which you'll be able to rely on.

My predecessor was very popular and I'm worried about stepping into her shoes. What's the best way of handling this?

Following someone into a job can be difficult whether they were popular or not: even if they weren't particularly well liked, people's expectations of you may be high and difficult to meet, which is an extra burden if you've just had a radical change of career. If you're following in the footsteps of a popular manager, though, don't write yourself off too soon! You are as yet untried and will be able to bring a new, fresh perspective to the job. However, it is still worth finding out what your predecessor did well, so that you know what your team responds to best, and then ask them what they'd like from you as their boss. Everyone likes to feel consulted, so this open approach will always be appreciated.

Step two: Prepare

Preparing as well as you can before you start your new job can make all the difference as you get through your first week. Feeling on top of your game will boost your confidence and make sure that you get the most from your early days.

You've probably done a lot of the hard work already as part of your job campaign, when you were researching your new employer ahead of interview, so revisit the information you compiled previously to refresh your memory about:

- your new employer organisation's structure
- strategy
- how they look after their staff
- any recent developments (such as acquisitions, major new deals, and so on)

One good source of information will be any press releases stored on your new company's website.

Although your main focus should, of course, be on looking to the future, it's no bad think to reflect on your past jobs and think about some of the lessons you've learned, good and bad. Are there any personal traits you want to leave behind? These could be anything from being prone to over-worry, taking comments personally, not listening to others well — you name it. Be honest and set yourself some goals that involve leaving behind these traits in your new job.

On a more prosaic level, you also need to know your start date, where you need to report to, and who you'll be meeting on your first day. Ask your new company to send through some logistical details via e-mail or letter so that you know what to expect on your first day. It's even worth asking your contact at your new employer if there is anything specific that you can do to prepare – if nothing else, this makes a great impression!

Step three: Ask for your objectives

On your first day, ask the person who is inducting you (most likely, this will be your line manager) to explain what you will initially be doing during your first week. It's a good idea to find out how you'll be introduced to your new colleagues (will you be formally introduced to them, or do they take a more relaxed approach?), as this will help you work out how best to integrate into the team.

Also, ask what your overall and long term objectives are at the outset, and what the timelines are. Once you're into the day to day details of a job, it's all too easy to lose sight of the bigger picture — this is especially the case if you've moved industry, when you'll be taking on new information by the bucketload on several fronts — so setting out your objectives is always a useful way of creating a point of reference that you can refer to in future. Do make sure that you revisit and review those objectives at regular intervals!

Step four: Remember people's names

It sounds simple and obvious, yet it is something that we all know can make a great impression — or a terrible one, if you get it wrong. If you're new job involves managing other people, it's essential that you build rapport with your staff, and remembering their names is the most basic way of doing so.

TOP TIP

Some people genuinely have a dreadful memory for names. If you know you're weak in this area, do something about it! There are lots of systems you can try (such as those using association) that can help you improve your memory. As a start, try visiting:

www.mindtools.com/pages/article/newTIM_12.htm

Step five: Don't rely on other people to integrate you

Although it's likely that your new manager will do the initial round of introductions when you start your new job, it's essential that you're proactive too. Often, other employees can be a bit wary of new recruits (especially new managers) and may be reticent about introducing themselves. Make sure you play your part and get to know them off your own bat. If you want to be regarded as an approachable and sociable manager or employee, show that you're willing to put the effort in as soon as you start work at your new company.

Step six: Observe

Your first week in a new job is likely to be the one and only point at which you can observe the working environment with genuine objectivity: it won't be long before you become aware of your new employer's expectations and 'the way things are done around here'. While you have the chance, use your fresh perspective to your advantage and observe your colleagues and the culture without emotional involvement. Also take the time to look at your surroundings and make a note of any elements or issues that may play a big role in how your role works or (if you've taken on a managerial role) how you can get the best from your team. For example, are your colleagues clear about what they're doing? Do they seem under stress or, at the other end of the spectrum, bored and detached? That said, try not to jump to conclusions or generalise: once you've been in your role for a few weeks, ask some discreet questions that will help you back up your initial findings or put them in better context.

Common Mistakes

✗ You try to make changes straight away
Though it is great to have ideas for making improvements, being overly critical about your new organisation, team, or surroundings in your first week is guaranteed to rub people up the wrong way. Yes, you might think that you're just offering some objective advice or solutions, and yes, being a proactive member of the team is very valuable. The key to success, however, is offering these insights in a way that will be welcomed. Remember that your new colleagues don't know or trust you yet, so it's wise to keep a note of issues you've spotted and then raise them at an appropriate time.

Use the first week as a time to ask questions, observe how things are done, and fully understand the processes in place. Even though some systems or processes may seem a bit unwieldy to you, find out why things are done that way — there could be a good reason. Be diplomatic and non-aggressive when you ask questions like this (people can feel under attack and become defensive), and phrase your queries carefully.

✗ **You don't adapt to your new work culture**
However keen you are to start a new job, you're bound to bring with you a bit of the mindset you developed at your last employer. This isn't always a bad thing, of course, but guard against any temptation you may feel to try to recreate your previous workplace. It just won't work, and the upshot will be that you'll feel unsettled and your new colleagues will feel slighted. You will need to adapt, so be ready to mould yourself and your skills to your new surroundings rather than expecting every-one to change to suit you!

Useful links

Chartered Institute of Managers:
www.managers.org.uk
iVillage:
www.ivillage.co.uk/workcareer
Monster:
www.monster.co.uk

Index